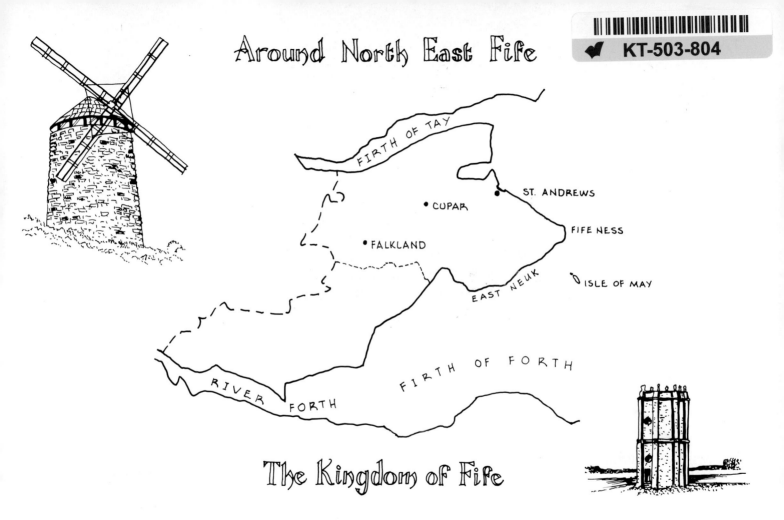

Around North East Fife

FIRTH OF TAY

• CUPAR

ST. ANDREWS

FIFE NESS

• FALKLAND

EAST NEUK

ꝺ ISLE OF MAY

FIRTH OF FORTH

RIVER FORTH

The Kingdom of Fife

The First edition of this book
was printed in February, 1992.
ISBN 0 9519134 0 9
Second Revised Edition - March 1997
ISBN 1 900651 00 9

THE BANNET STANE, WEST LOMOND.

Handwritten text and illustrations by John M Pearson
© Copyright JMP. All rights reserved - 1997
A catalogue record for this book is available
from the British Library.

Printed by :-
Levenmouth Printers
Banbeath Place
Leven, Fife.

Around North East Fife

FALKLAND PALACE

by John M. Pearson

4 Mercat Cross, Cupar.

The Kingdom of Fife still proudly retains its identity and over the centuries this has been reinforced by the geographical factors which have tended to isolate Fife. Projecting out into the North Sea, Fife is protected to the north by the Firth of Tay, to the south by the Firth of Forth and to the west by the Ochil Hills. Within these boundaries Fife has flourished and the Fly Fifers have developed a distinct identity which commands a healthy respect from other Scots as acknowledged in the saying :-

"It taks a lang spune tae sup wi' a Fifer."

The first edition of this book concentrated on the more popular and larger towns and villages around North-east Fife. The second edition also includes many of the smaller villages which contribute to the character and history of this area. Starting in the East Neuk there are the quaint fishing villages that hug the coast between Largo and Fife Ness. Further round the coast is St. Andrews, famous for its religious and historical influence on Scottish affairs; its role in founding the first University in Scotland and its position as the headquarters of world golf. Cupar, the old county town is centrally situated and further west in the Howe of Fife, sheltering in the shadow of the Lomond Hills, are the Royal town of Falkland, Auchtermuchty, Strathmiglo, Freuchie and Gateside. To the north along the River Tay are Newburgh, the ruined abbey of Balmerino and the old ferry ports to Dundee.

The first port of call is Largo with one village - Lower Largo - concentrated around the harbour area and the other - Upper Largo - situated further inland at the foot of Largo Law. The Parish Church of Upper Largo is easily identifiable as it stands high on a knoll on the edge of the village. The Church has been established in Largo for over 1100 years and has undergone many changes. The most notable was the addition of the spire in 1628 which is supported rather unusually on the arched roof of the Chancel. Many interesting murals and stones may be seen in the Church and Church yard including the Largo Stone with its Celtic engravings. Beyond Upper Largo rises Largo Law (294m) and stories of buried treasure on the Law have filtered down through the centuries. In 1819 a tinker proved the stories were fact, not fiction when he unearthed Celtic silver ornaments on nearby Norries Law. Unfortunately the silver was melted down but further excavations found more Celtic ornaments which are now safely on display in the National Museum in Edinburgh.

The origin of the three large Standing Stones on the Lundin Ladies Golf Course is unknown but the most plausible theory is that the five metre high stones may well represent the remains of a stone circle as used by the Druids. Several stone cists were uncovered close by and these date back nearly 2000 years. Within sight of the stones is the 16th century ruined tower of Lundie House which was the mansion house of the Lundin family. Lundin Links is mainly a holiday resort and the Lundin Links Golf Club is one of many first class courses to be found in the North East Fife area.

Upper Largo Kirk

5

Crusoe Hotel, Lower Largo.

Lower Largo is the home of the legendary Robinson Crusoe whose adventures were portrayed in a novel by Daniel Defoe. Crusoe's exploits were based on the real life adventure of Alexander Selkirk whose unruly behaviour at sea caused his Captain to put him ashore on the deserted island of Juan Fernandez in the Pacific Ocean. Selkirk survived for four years before being rescued and the statue in Main Street is quite appropriate with Selkirk looking hopefully out to sea in search of a ship. The statue marks the site of the cottage where Selkirk was born in 1676.

Robinson Crusoe's adventures have left their mark in Lower Largo and the old mid 19th century granary at the harbour is now the Crusoe Hotel. It was extended in 1991 and has an information and display area on Alexander Selkirk which gives an account of his adventurous life along with several seafaring items of interest.

The other famous seafarer from Largo is Sir Andrew Wood (1460 - 1540) who was Captain of the warship Yellow Carvel and a valued counsellor of James III & IV. His most famous victory took place in 1498 when he trounced the invading English fleet which ventured into the Firth of Forth. Wood was knighted for his exploits and also received the lands of Largo upon which he built a castle. Sir Andrew Wood now lies buried in Largo Church and the remains of the canal running from his residence to the Church may still be seen.

The Alexander Selkirk / Robinson Crusoe Statue

7

Town Hall,
Earlsferry

In contrast to the compact harbours of the other east neuk Fishing ports Elie harbour sweeps round in a wide arc into Ruby Bay. The Old Granary building stands at the end of the pier overlooking a harbour that has severely declined in trade and fishing since the heydays of the 1800's. Prior to that Elie was made a Burgh of Barony in 1589 and then combined with Earlsferry in 1929. Today Elie and Earlsferry are primarily residential seaside resorts.

Earlsferry gained its name from an incident connected with the escape of Macduff, the Thane or Earl of Fife from Macbeth in the eleventh century. Macduff had hidden in a cave near to Kincraig Point until it was possible for local fishermen to take him safely over the Firth of Forth to Dunbar - thus giving the place a simple but apt name of Earlsferry.

In Elie High Street the old parish church is a prominent landmark. It was built in 1639 by Sir William Scott of Ardross Castle and the octagonal clock tower was added later in 1726 by Sir John Anstruther. Another connection with the Anstruther family is the Lady's Tower which was built on the cliffs to the east of the town. It was used as a summer house by Janet Fall, the Lady Anstruther of Elie House.

Lady Janet obviously loved her privacy and when she went swimming in the sea a bellman was sent through the streets of Elie to warn any curious townfolk to keep their distance. She was also responsible for raising the hamlet of Balclevie to the ground in order to improve the view.

In the old part of Elie, Gillespie House in South Street was rebuilt in 1870 but retained the doorway of the Muckle Yett - named after the 'Big Gate' of an earlier house on this site. The date 1682 and the initials of Alex. Gillespie and his wife Christina Small are carved in a marriage lintel over the door.

Elie and Earlsferry have notable golf links. The most famous golfer from this airt was James Braid who won the British Open Championship five times between 1901 and 1910. Crossing Earlsferry links is the old Cadger's Road which was named after the cadgers or carriers who took fresh fish to the Royal Palace of Falkland.

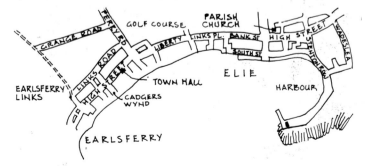

Elie Parish Church

9

The East Neuk of Fife refers in particular to the small fishing communities located between Largo Bay and Fife Ness. These old communities huddle precariously around the harbours and even today their charm and character is still retained due to the preservation of many of the little houses by the National Trust for Scotland.

In earlier days the East Neuk communities all benefited from the fishing industry and trade with the Low Countries. Consequently Crail and Pittenweem had separate market places for trading and they were located away from the harbours at the top of the cliffs. Until early this century the North Sea herring shoals had revived the prosperity of the East Neuk fishing ports. With the decline of the herring the ports were subsequently affected and today only Pittenweem thrives as a busy fishing port.

THE EAST NEUK

PEAT INN
LARGO-WARD
LARGO LAW 311m
KELLIE CASTLE
UPPER LARGO
COLINSBURGH
BALCASKIE
KILCONQUHAR
LOWER LARGO
ELIE
EARLSFERRY
LARGO BAY

FIFE NESS
CRAIL
KILRENNY
CELLARDYKE
ANSTRUTHER
PITTENWEEM
ST MONANS
ISLE OF MAY

FIRTH OF FORTH

10   Pittenweem Harbour

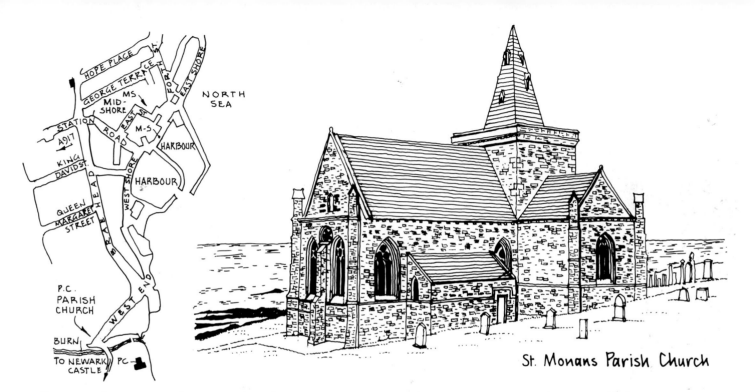

St. Monans Parish Church

Originally named Inverin, St. Monans took its present name from the remains of St. Moineinn which were reputedly brought over from Ireland by the early Christian missionaries. They established a shrine near the site of the present Church on the shore. In 1362 King David II worshipped at the shrine to give thanks for his survival after his ship was wrecked in the Firth of Forth. To express his gratitude he ordered a Church to be built and its distinctive squat appearance is now a landmark on the edges of the shore. Inside the Church the strong connection with the sea is depicted by a hanging model of a late 18th century sailing ship.   The Church was in ruins in the 1770's and between 1826-28 major restoration work was carried out under the supervision of architect William Burns.

11

West Shore, St. Monans.

A few hundred yards beyond the Church are the ruins of Newark Castle, formerly the home of the Abercrombies. In 1649 the Castle was bought by General David Leslie, who became the first Lord Newark in 1661. Leslie's most notable victory was at Philiphaugh in 1645 where he defeated the Marquis of Montrose and his army. As a mark of respect Leslie was buried within St. Monans Church but during the alterations in 1828 his remains were ditched into the sea by mistake.

Alongside the Castle ruins is one of the best surviving examples of a 16th century doocot. This particular doocot is unusual in that it is in the shape of a beehive and has been recently restored by the East Neuk of Fife Preservation Society. The standard doocot is of a rectangular design with a lean-to slate roof and is a familiar landmark in Fife. They were built by the lairds to house doos or doves to ensure a fresh supply of meat during the long winter months.

Beyond Newark Castle lies the very fragmented ruin of Ardross Castle which was built in 1370 by the Dishington family. The houses opposite are typical of the fishing villages with their crowstepped gables, pantiles, dormer windows and forestair allowing access to the first floor and providing storage under.

St. Monans Harbour

The old fishing village of St. Monans perches precariously along the shoreline and hugs the harbour wall for protection from the Firth of Forth. As with all East Neuk ports St. Monans relied on the fishing industry but also diversified into coal mining and salt working until the early 1800's. After that the herring industry briefly revived the town's fortunes and the harbour was improved to cope with the extra trade. Boat building was also a flourishing industry and until recently the firm of James N. Millar & Sons, founded in 1747, had been involved in boatbuilding in St. Monans since 1779. To the east of St. Monans the East Neuk of Fife Preservation Society and Fife Council have restored a windmill built in the 1770's. Interpretation panels indicate the process whereby the windmill pumped sea water into the salt pans below and the coal fires heated the water until evaporation took place. The salt deposits were then gathered up and shipped out from Pittenweem.

13

Kellie Lodging, Pittenweem.

Pittenweem is a Celtic name meaning town of the cave which refers to the Cave in Cove Wynd. This was used as a place of worship by the 7th century missionary St. Fillan and legend tells of the mysterious light which used to glow from his left arm allowing him to see and write in the dark cave. St. Fillans cave was restored in 1935 and inside there is an altar and the Saint's Well. A staircase from the cave used to lead up to the Priory Gardens nearby but it is now sealed off.

When the Augustinian Priory was moved from the Isle of May to Pittenweem the town developed around the Priory and eventually became a Royal Burgh in 1541. The High Street has a wide treelined market area with the 16th century Parish Church and Tolbooth forming a focal point at one end. The Tolbooth tower contains the Council Chamber at first floor level with a dungeon in the basement. In more superstitious times many a witch was held here awaiting trial by the enthusiastic local witch-hunters.

The Mercat Cross, normally located in the Market Place now stands inappropriately alongside the tower. The impressive Kellie Lodging in the High Street was built in the 1590's. It was the Town House of the Earls of Kellie who owned the nearby Kellie Castle.

Behind the High Street in Routine Row a plaque tells the story about James Stark, an exciseman who was robbed by an Andrew Wilson and George Robertson in 1736. The two men were caught and tried and their attempted escape in Edinburgh on the way to their execution led to the infamous Porteous Riots. From the High Street several wynds weave their way down through the huddled houses to the harbour which is presently the busiest in all the East Neuk. Consequently Pittenweem is well equipped to deal with all the requirements of a busy fishing industry. Most mornings the fish catches are sold at the covered fish market on the quay and further along the coast an old granary houses an ice factory for storing the fish.

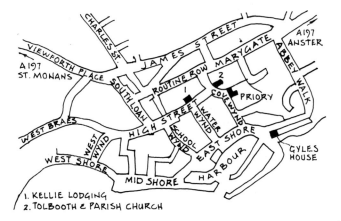

1. KELLIE LODGING
2. TOLBOOTH & PARISH CHURCH

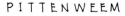

PITTENWEEM

Pittenweem with the Isle of May on the horizon 15

Gyles House, Pittenweem.

The Isle of May lies six miles off the East Neuk guarding the entrance to the Firth of Forth. It was originally a base for the early Christian missionaries, one of whom was St. Adrian who became the patron saint of many of the East Neuk ports. The Isle of May was always open to continuous attacks from raiding Norsemen and St. Adrian was murdered by the Danes in one such attack about 875 A.D.

David I founded a priory here in the 12th century but again the Norsemen forced the missionaries to retreat to Pittenweem where they founded another priory. The Isle of May has had a lighthouse for over 350 years and the remains of the Mayfire Tower can still be seen. It was built in 1636 and was the first lighthouse built in Scotland.

The Royal Burgh of Anstruther gained its charter in 1587 and comprises Easter and Wester Anstruther, which are separated by the Dreel Burn, and nearby Cellardyke. The Parish Church of St. Adrian was built in 1634. Its location on the slopes of School Green give it a good vantage point in Wester Anstruther and the spire and tower are easily seen over the houses crowding around the harbour. Nearby in Back Dykes is the Old Manse built in 1590 by James Melville whose diaries give a fascinating account of life in medieval Scotland. Archbishop James Sharp was known to shelter here on his fateful journey across Magus Muir. St. Adrian's Parish Church Hall stands alongside the Town Hall of Easter Anstruther down by the Dreel Burn. Opposite is the Buckie House with its gable decorated with patterns of scallop shells and buckies.

Anstruther harbour was one of the busiest ports in Scotland but the decline of the herring affected the town's prosperity as well as the rest of the East Neuk. In spite of this Anstruther still retains a strong link with its past and tucked in at the eastern end of the harbour is the Scottish Fisheries Museum. It was opened in 1969 and won the Museum of the Year Award for Scotland in 1976.

The Scottish Fisheries Museum, Anstruther.

17

The Reaper, Anstruther.

The Museum displays a well documented record of the fishing community in days gone by and is located at St. Ayles land. This is one of the oldest properties of any Scottish burgh with a charter dating back to 1318. The east side of the property was the 16th century lodgings for the monks who travelled from Balmerino Abbey in North Fife to buy their fish.

The Museum purchased the old boatyard in East Shore, which was the last remaining boatbuilding yard in Anstruther. The boat yard is now used as a museum to display a collection of fifteen boats. As well as displays on the fishing industry the Museum includes other attractions such as a restored wheelhouse, a fisherman's house, a fish-monger's shop and a collection of paintings along with a large photographic archive. It also houses the Memorial to Scottish Fishermen Lost at Sea.

Out in the harbour lies the 'Reaper' one of the Fifie herring boats meticulously restored by the Museum. Plans are presently underway to build a new museum by the harbour to exhibit the 'Research' which was one of the revolutionary designed Zulu Drifter herring boats.

Famous folk from Anstruther include Dr. Thomas Chalmers, and the cottage where he was born in 1780 is still standing in the High Street. Chalmers became a stalwart of the Church and was the First Moderator of the Assembly of the Free Church of Scotland. Another person of note was Lieutenant Andrew Waid who bequeathed his fortune in 1804 to the establishment of Waid Academy for the benefit of local education. Finally there was William Tennant (1784 - 1848) who became a Professor in Oriental Languages at St. Andrews University. In 1812 he published a poem called 'Anster Fair.' It had great local appeal and told the story of a local lass, Maggie Lauder and her courting days in the 16th century.

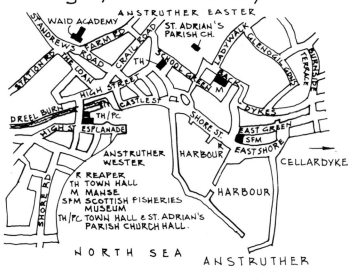

Town Hall and St. Adrian's Parish Church Hall,
Anstruther.

19

Cellardyke harbour

The quaint old fishing village of Cellardyke was previously named Nether Kilrenny and Skinfasthaven because the fishing folk from Kilrenny kept their tackle in cellars near the harbour. They also built stone dykes around the drying greens at the top of the cliffs to protect the nets from animals – hence the name Cellardyke. The harbour was rebuilt between 1829-31 but is mainly used by pleasurecraft now as the fishing industry has declined. Cellardyke has its own Town Hall built in 1883 and alongside stands the octagonal shaft of the old Mercat Cross dated 1642. To the east of the harbour is the local outdoor bathing pool known as the 'Cardinal Steps' after Cardinal David Beaton of St. Andrews who had a seaside residence at Pitmilly in the 16th century.

20

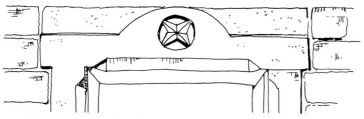

Carved door lintel

Kilrenny is a small village to the north of Anstruther and dominated by the Parish Church which was built in 1808. The first religious building in the area was a chapel dedicated to the Irish missionary St. Ethernan in 864 AD. Another church was built in 1243 which survived until 1808 when it was demolished to make way for the present church.

The 18th century tomb of the Lumisdaines family of Innergelly stands near the church tower. The most famous member was Sir James Lumisdaines who fought with distinction for Gustavus Adolphus of Sweden. It is also believed that the remains of the murdered Cardinal David Beaton lie near the Kilrenny church - secretly buried to avoid the wrath of his enemies.

In 1578 Kilrenny was given a charter to hold a weekly fair and although these days are long gone the village still retains its old charm.

Parish Church, Kilrenny

Crail is the oldest of the East Neuk burghs and became a Royal Burgh in the 12th century. In 1310 Crail received Royal permission from Robert the Bruce to hold Sunday markets. These were held in the treelined Marketgate where the 17th century Mercat Cross with its unicorn now stands. Nearby is the 16th century Tolbooth with its council chamber, court room and prison alongside the Town Hall which was built later in 1814. The weathervane on top of the Tolbooth has a fish representing the famous local Crail capon – a haddock that was either smoked or dried in the sun. Just below is the Tolbooth bell, which is still tolled at 10.00 pm every day, except Sundays, to signal the local curfew. Crail Museum, which opened in 1979 is also in the Marketgate and is run by the Crail Preservation Trust. It displays the history of the Royal Burgh of Crail including trade, local crafts, golf and the activities of the nearby airport which was the Royal Naval Air Station during the Second World War and intriguingly called H.M.S. Jackdaw.

Alongside the Town Kirk of St. Marys lies a large blue stone reputedly thrown at the Kirk from the Isle of May by Auld Nick, the devil. There has been a church on this site since the 12th century making it one of the oldest religious places in Scotland. The churchyard contains a mort house that was used to thwart notorious bodysnatchers of the early 1800's.

Mercat Cross, Crail

From the High Street the Shoregate leads down to the small harbour which is enclosed on two sides by traditional east neuk domestic buildings and the larger 17th century crow stepped Customs House. The harbour presents a very picturesque scene which is more evident when viewed from the West Braes. As has happened elsewhere in the East Neuk Crail harbour now sees little activity compared to yesteryear. Even with its marketplace which encouraged many crafts in the area there has been a large decline in both trade and fishing.

Crail Golfing Society is the seventh oldest golf club in the world. Unlike many old established clubs it has managed to keep a complete set of minutes from its foundation on 23rd February 1786 until the present day.

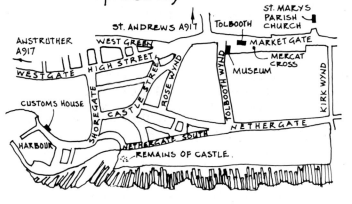

CRAIL

The Tolbooth, Crail.

The Square, Kingsbarns.

In the Middle Ages the old village of North Barns was surrounded by some of the finest farming land in the country and renowned for its grain production. The Kings of Scots were quick to capitalise on this and acquired the great village barns for storing their grain to use at the Royal Court at Crail and Falkland. Consequently the village was given the royal prefix and has been known as Kingsbarns ever since.

In the 16th century, James V, a frequent visitor to Falkland Palace granted a charter to Kingsbarns on condition that the village folk would join the Royal army. His son, James VI then gave the lands in his dowry to his wife Queen Anne of Denmark before transferring them to his old nurse, Helen Little. Today the local church, built in 1631 and enlarged in 1810 dominates the village square which still has the old water pump dated 1831.

Town Hall, Colinsburgh

Sundial on skewputt of house in North Wynd, Colinsburgh.

Most of the villages along the east neuk are located on the coast which provides their livelihood, but the village of Colinsburgh lies inland and almost due north of Kilconquhar Loch. The reason for this is that the village was specifically built by Colin, the 3rd Earl of Balcarres in 1705. This Fife nobleman was a fervent supporter of the Jacobites and between 1693-1700 he was in exile in Holland with his fellow supporters.

On his return to Scotland he founded the village of Colinsburgh and built cottages to house his disbanded soldiers. During the 1715 Rebellion Colin again supported the Jacobite cause which eventually floundered after an inconclusive battle at Sheriffmuir. Harsh sentences were imposed on the rebels but luckily for Colin he escaped with a light sentence and was confined to his quarters at Balcarres House near Colinsburgh.

25

26   The Parish Church, Kilconquhar.

Main Street, Kilconquhar

At the picturesque village of Kilconquhar the nearby loch is a favourite haunt of wildlife but in winter when the water is frozen over the loch resounds to the noise and enthusiasm of the roaring game of curling. The loch forms a spectacular setting for the early 19th century Parish Church which sits high on a knoll above both the loch and village. There has been a church at Kilconquhar since the early 12th century and legend maintains that witches were drowned in the loch as a punishment for their evil and wicked ways. An old ballad tells of the trials of a notorious witch of Pittenweem :-

"They tied her hands behind her back
An' twisted them wi' a pin
An' they dragged her to Kilconquhar loch
An' coupit the limmer in."

Kilconquhar has many 18th and 19th century vernacular houses which add a touch of character to the streets. To the east of the village stands Kilconquhar House and the ruins of a 16th century castle which was partially destroyed by fire in 1978. Since then the castle has been restored and forms the focal point for the time-share holiday homes on the estate.

27

Kellie Castle

In the 11th century the Barony of Kellie was the principal seat of the Saxon family of Seward and Kellie Castle, standing in the shadow of Kellie Law, was built later about 1360. It was then that the estate passed to Sir Walter Oliphant whose family ran the estate for over 200 years before it passed through various hands including Thomas Erskine who became the First Earl of Kellie in 1619.

Originally Kellie Castle was a tower or keep and between 1573-1605 it was enlarged to its present design with an enchanting three dimensional display of corbels, crowstepped gables, chimneys and dormer windows. In 1829 the Castle was abandoned and fell into neglect. In the 1870's James Lorimer rented the Castle as a summer house and started on the internal restorations which was an ongoing process even after the Lorimer Family bought the Castle in 1948. James' son, Robert was the successful architect and responsible for the design of the Thistle Chapel at St. Giles and the National War Memorial in Edinburgh Castle. Inside Kellie Castle there is an exhibition in memory of his work. In 1970 the National Trust for Scotland purchased Kellie Castle and Gardens in the interests of preserving yet another property for the nation.

Balcaskie House

Balcaskie House was rebuilt by architect Sir William Bruce who bought the Balcaskie Estate in 1665. He carried out major alterations to the existing house and his formal design of the terraces and gardens was an innovation in Scotland.

The design was centred around the Bass Rock in the Firth of Forth which acted as a focal point. Sir William Bruce sold the Balcaskie Estate in 1684 to Sir Thomas Stewart of Grandtully and in 1698 it was then sold to Sir Robert Anstruther. Since then nine generations of the Anstruther family have inherited the estate and today it is owned by Sir Ralph H. Anstruther of that Ilk, Bart.

29

St. Andrews Cathedral

St. Andrews - the jewel in the Kingdom of Fife - a city that has played a major role in Scottish religious history, in Scottish education and in the international world of golf was founded on the legend that the bones of St. Andrew were brought to the old township of Kilrymont over 1000 years ago. Adopting the new name of St. Andrews, the town soon became a centre for pilgrims who came to worship the remains of the Patron Saint for Scotland. From as early as the sixth century religion had a strong influence in the development of St. Andrews with the Celtic Church on Kirkhill being founded by the Culdees. The founding of the Cathedral and Priory in 1160 was a major step in establishing St. Andrews as an ecclesiastical centre which played a dominant role in boosting the development and importance of the town.

The Castle was built later around 1200 for the protection of the Bishops and during 400 turbulent years was destroyed and rebuilt many times. The history of the Castle is a cruel one and reflects desperate times in medieval Scotland. In the ruined Sea Tower is the infamous Bottle Dungeon; its bottle shape hewn out of the rock thus making escape impossible. Among the many prisoners held here in the dark dank conditions were the martyrs Walter Myln, Patrick Hamilton and George Wishart.

The Church placed great emphasis on education and was instrumental in establishing the first University in St. Andrews and indeed in Scotland in 1410. The First University buildings to be built were the College and Church of St. Salvator which were founded in 1450 by Bishop James Kennedy - renowned as one of the great Scots of his era. Future development included the founding of St. Leonard's College in 1512 and St. Mary's College in 1538.

The period prior to the Reformation in 1559 was a particularly cruel one and markings in the cobbled streets at Deans Court, St. Salvator's College and Market Street all indicate where the martyrs were burned at the stake for their religious beliefs. The Reformation was to signal the end of St. Andrews as a dominant religious force in Scotland. Consequently both the Castle and Cathedral declined in importance and fell into ruin.

Initially the University helped to sustain the importance of St. Andrews but throughout the next two centuries the University lurched in the doldrums. In 1876 the University took the unprecedented step of encouraging women to enrol as students to boost their recruitment drive. It was a success and proved once again that St. Andrews University was one of the leaders in the field of education.

The Bell Tower at St. Mary's College

32

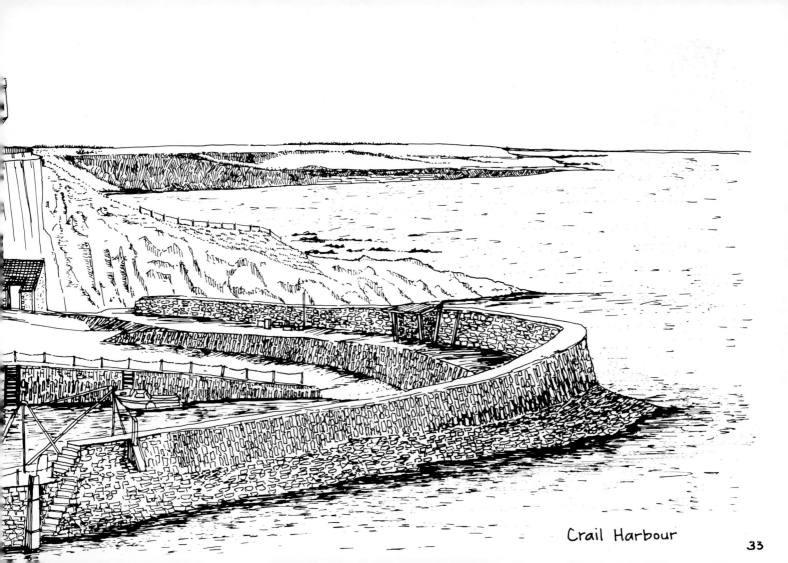

Crail Harbour

33

The Royal and Ancient Golf Clubhouse.

BRITISH GOLF MUSEUM

R&A
1

9

NORTH SEA

GOLF ROAD

ST. SALVATORS COLLEGE

THE SCORES

CASTLE

NORTH STREET

CITY ROAD

MARKET STREET

8

HOLY TRINITY CHURCH

5

6

ST. MARY-ON-THE-ROCK

WEST PORT

SOUTH STREET

7

HARBOUR

THE PENDS

2

3 4

BYRE THEATRE

ST. LEONARDS

ABBEY

MILL PORT

MADRAS COLLEGE

1 ROYAL & ANCIENT GOLF CLUB
2 BLACKFRIARS CHAPEL
3 TOWN HALL
4 ST. MARY'S COLLEGE
5 PRESERVATION TRUST MUSEUM

6 . CATHEDRAL & MUSEUM
7 . ST. RULES TOWER
8 . ST. ANDREWS MUSEUM
9 . SEALIFE CENTRE

ST. ANDREWS

Golf or gowf was another factor which drove St. Andrews into national and international fame. As far back as the 15th century it was noted that James II banned golf so that men could concentrate fully on their archery practice. Eventually the ever increasing popularity of golf called for some form of framework to control the evolution of the game. This was achieved by the formation of the Society of St. Andrews Golfers on 14th May, 1754. When King William IV was nominated as Patron in 1834 the name was changed to the Royal and Ancient Golf Club of St. Andrews. The Clubhouse was built in 1854 and today the R&A is recognised as the headquarters of world golf and is responsible for organising the Open Championships throughout Britain.

St. Andrews is fortunate in that the medieval street plan is still intact and many of the buildings which contribute to the character of the town still remain. Since Provost Sir Hugh Lyon Playfair improved the town in the mid 19th century there has been a conscious effort to preserve the heritage of St. Andrews. Museums and other places of interest worth visiting include the British Golf Museum, St. Andrews Museum at Kinburn House, St. Andrews Preservation Trust Museum in North Street, the Cathedral Museum and St. Rules Tower, the Castle, Town Hall, Holy Trinity Church, the Sealife Centre in the Scores and Craigtoun Park situated just outside St. Andrews.

Magus Muir - "History broods over that part of the Kingdom like the easterly haar" wrote Robert Louis Stevenson......and the gruesome scenes that took place on 3rd May 1679 are today marked by a simple stone pyramid that stands amidst the trees of Bishop's Wood on Magus Muir. The pyramid marks the scene of the murder of Archbishop James Sharp of St. Andrews by a band of Covenanters. They were hiding on Magus Muir to ambush Sheriff Carmichael of Fife but it was the Archbishop Sharp who blundered into their hands. He was dragged from his stagecoach and brutally murdered in front of his daughter - and all the while, Hackston of Rathillet sat on horseback in the background, his cloak drawn over his mouth as he watched the gory proceedings.

For his role in the murder Hackston was cruelly executed the following year in Edinburgh and parts of his body were displayed in St. Andrews, Magus Muir, Cupar, Burntisland, Leith and Glasgow. This was to act as a deterrent to those who sought to oppose the might of the Catholic Church.

A large tomb surrounded by railings lies near to the stone pyramid and contains the remains of five men who also "suffered martyrdom on Magus Muir for their adherence to the word of God and Scotland's Covenant of Reformation."

Pyramid Memorial on Magus Muir -

St. Salvator's College

DI - DUNCAN INSTITUTE. CE-CORN EXCHANGE.
CB-COUNTY BUILDINGS. M - MARKET.

C U P A R (See page 44)

St. Athernase Church, Leuchars.

The original church at Leuchars was built about 1183 and is recognised as one of the best examples of Norman architecture in Scotland. In 1244 the church was dedicated to St. Athernase by Bishop de Bernham of St. Andrews. Over the centuries there have been many alterations and extensions to the old church. In 1745 the present stone bell tower replaced the original roof and then a new nave was added later in 1857.

At the south door are memorial stones to the Bruces of Earlshall including one to Sir William Bruce who fought at Flodden in 1513 and later founded Earlshall. Near the pulpit is a memorial to Robert Carnegie of Kinnaird who was ambassador to both Mary de Guise and Mary Queen of Scots. In 1987 the standard of III Fighter Squadron from RAF Leuchars was put on display in the chancel to mark over 800 years in the church's history.

36

Surprisingly there is no memorial to Alexander Henderson who was the greatest minister ever to be associated with Leuchars. Henderson started his career as a minister at Leuchars in 1612 and was elected Moderator of the General Assembly at Glasgow Cathedral in 1638. Shortly afterwards he moved to St. Giles in Edinburgh and died there nine years later from marsh fever – an illness contracted from the marshes in the Leuchars area.

The first Leuchars castle was built in the 12th century by Robert de Quincy – a Norman knight who settled in Scotland in 1175. This timber-built castle was located to the north of the church. It was replaced by a stone castle which was demolished in the late 18th century.

Today Leuchars is renowned for its RAF base and its popular Battle of Britain air displays held every September. It was back in 1911 that the Royal Engineers first experimented with the use of balloons at Leuchars. Later the Royal Navy established the Fleet Training School and built an airfield. In 1920 the RAF then took control and RAF Leuchars is a vital part of Britain's defences.

Near Leuchars is the village of Guardbridge – aptly named as there are bridges over the River Eden and Mottray Water. The oldest bridge with its six arches and triangular cutwaters was built in the early 15th century by Bishop Henry Wardlaw. Stone panels are visible on either side of the bridge with the north panel depicting the arms and initials of Archbishop James Beaton (1522-39). Today, however, it is the 'modern' bridge built in 1935-37 that carries the traffic to and from St. Andrews.

The name Guardbridge reputedly derives from the English word 'yard' referring to an enclosure. In this instance the 'yard' is most likely the area between the bridges and two rivers. In 1873 the Guardbridge Paper Company Ltd. was established and transformed this hamlet into a thriving industrial village centred around the paper mill. From the late 1890's the marshy land between the River Eden and Mottray Burn has been reclaimed to allow the mill to expand and cater for modern requirements. Today the paper mill is run by Curtis Fine Papers Group which also has another Scottish mill at Dalmore and their products are sold all over the world.

38 The River Eden at Guardbridge

Earlshall Castle was built in 1546 by Sir William Bruce and after falling into decay it was magnificently restored by Sir Robert Lorimer between 1891 - 1898. Today it is the private family home of the Baron and Baroness of Earlshall and is open to the public at certain times during the year. Inside, the Long Gallery has a painted ceiling which depicts the arms of the principal families in Scotland and countless mythological beasts. The walls below are decorated with an impressive array of over one hundred Scottish broadswords as a reminder of Scotland's warlike past. The Dining Room at First Floor level has an oak balustrade screen and Lorimer based this design on a similar screen at Falkland Palace. In the Rod and Gun Room there is a collection of antique firearms and fishing tackle and throughout the Castle there are many interesting items of antique furniture, porcelain and paintings on display. In 1561 Mary Queen of Scots visited Earlshall Castle and her bedchamber may still be seen complete with the furnishings of that period.

The Castle forms an open courtyard with a small 16th century tower, the coachman's house and stables which lead to the gardens with the famous topiary yews which are trimmed into the shape of chessmen. The approach to the Castle is protected by the massive Gatehouse built in 1900 by Sir Robert Lorimer.

Earlshall Castle

Ex Parish Church, now the Community Centre, Tayport.

The Ferry routes from north Fife across to Dundee have been long established and Ferryport-on-Craig, known simply as Tayport since 1846, is one of the oldest ports, mainly linking up with Broughty Ferry on the far side. This was the route that Macduff took nearly 900 years ago as once again he fled from the clutches of Macbeth. During the reign of James II the strategic importance of Tayport was recognised and a Castle was built to protect the entrance to the Firth of Tay. Today, only the street name of Castle Road hints at the presence of a Castle which was demolished long ago.

Tayport benefited from its association with Dundee and the arrival of the railway and the rebuilding of the harbour in 1847 made Tayport into a thriving industrial port. The building of the Tay Rail Bridge threatened Tayport's existence and eventually the port declined in importance with the last ferry crossing in 1939. Competition had always threatened ferry communities and further west, Woodhaven was a popular crossing in medieval times. Famous folk such as the outlaw Rob Roy MacGregor had crossed here in 1715 and in 1773 the Englishman Dr. Samuel Johnson also used this ferry crossing. In his book he was obviously smarting at the cost of the ferry over to Dundee and he made scathing reference to the four shilling payment for such a short ferry crossing.

In 1715 a pier and inn were established at Seamylnes, later called New Dundee and now known as Newport-on-Tay. In 1823 further development was encouraged when the harbour was built for steamboats. Newport then became a fashionable 'suburb' of Dundee for the wealthy jute barons. Consequently the ferry service from Woodhaven was eventually phased out in the mid 19th century in the face of such competition.

The Tay Rail Bridge, designed by Engineer Thomas Bouch, was built between 1871-78. The bridge was over two miles long and had massive girders of over 80 metres in length. On 28th December 1879 the Edinburgh mail train set off across the bridge to Dundee as a fiercesome gale battered the high girders, which buckled and crashed into the River Tay. The train was doomed and plunged into the Tay killing all 75 people on board. Another rail bridge was built alongside between 1882-87 and at 3.5 kilometre long it was the longest bridge in the U.K. The stumps of the old bridge piers protrude above the water as a sinister reminder of the Tay Bridge disaster. The building of the Tay Road Bridge in 1966 coincided with the last ferry crossing between Dundee and Newport-on-Tay and another way of life had given way to progress.

Wormit owes its existence to the Tay Rail Bridge and has flourished as a 'commuter town' for Dundee. It is renowned for being the first village in Scotland to have electric light.

Drinking Fountain, 1882 at Newport-on-Tay with Tay Rail Bridge in the background.

41

Balmerino may well derive from the Gaelic 'Bal' meaning town and the name of 'Merinach' - an early Celtic Saint who visited the area. In 1229 Balmerino Abbey was founded by Queen Ermengarde, the wife of King William the Lion and a direct descendant of William the Conqueror. Balmerino may well have been chosen as the site for the Abbey because this hamlet was a ferry crossing point on the pilgrimage route between St. Andrews and Arbroath. Queen Ermengarde died in 1233 and was buried in front of the high altar which was later descecrated in more violent times. Balmerino was established as a daughterhouse of the Abbey of Melrose, the first Cistercian monastery in Scotland, and the monks of Melrose were involved in the original building. In the 13th century the monks added a south aisle then a chapter house was built on in the 15th century.

On Christmas night in 1547 an invading English raiding party attacked and set fire to Balmerino and the Abbey. The main stone structure of the Abbey survived and although the Abbey was soon repaired the Reformers ransacked the Abbey in 1559 and it gradually fell into ruin. In 1936 the Earl of Dundee donated the Abbey to the National Trust for Scotland who have been actively involved in restoring the Chapter House.

Balmullo derives from the Gaelic 'Bal' and 'mullach an tighe' meaning 'roof.' and so Balmullo is appropriately named 'top village' with extensive views from the side of Lucklawhill down to the coast. To the north of Balmullo the redstone quarry is a familiar landmark on the side of Lucklawhill. Quarrying started here in 1925 and the redstone chips are used in many locations throughout Fife. Balmullo's most famous citizen of yesteryear was a cartoonist, Martin Anderson, whose talents won him national fame under the name of 'Cynicus'. He was also involved in the first picture postcards which were produced in a factory at Tayport. Anderson lived in 'Cynicus Castle' - a folly built of local redstone but after his death in 1932 the Castle was demolished.

Abbey ruins

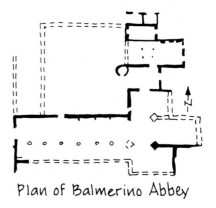

Plan of Balmerino Abbey

Dairsie is a village of 18th and 19th century weavers' cottages. It was also known as 'Osnaburgh' because of the connection with the osnaburg, which was a coarse linen cloth processed in the village. Many of the Dairsie weavers were Flemish and in 1823 they attempted to permanently change the village name to Osnaburgh but it came to nought. The two village names, however, are still printed side by side on road maps.

South of the village the 16th century Dairsie bridge spans the River Eden. On the east side of the bridge a stone panel displays the arms of James Beaton, Archbishop of St. Andrews from 1522-38. On top of the nearby hillock stands the Church of St. Mary's built by John Spottiswoode, Archbishop of St. Andrews, in 1621. The Church is a mixture of architectural styles and was designed with an unusual octagonal bell turret and stunted stone spire.

Beside the Church stands Dairsie Castle, home of the Learmouths of Dairsie in years gone by. David II, (1324-71) lived here for a while during his youth and in 1335 a meeting of the Scottish Estates was held at the Castle. After languishing in ruins for many years the Castle has recently been restored as a private residence.

St. Mary's (Old Parish) Church, Dairsie.

Cupar developed around the Castle of the Thanes of Fife and by 1328 achieved the status of a Royal Burgh. Its central location in Fife firmly established Cupar as a market centre and it was soon recognised as the County town of Fife with County buildings and Sheriff courts - hence the saying 'He that will to Cupar, maun to Cupar'. Today, Cupar is the administrative centre for the North-east Fife area of Fife Council.

In 1535 the first performance of Sir David Lindsay's play 'The Satire of the Three Estates' took place on Castlehill. The play cleverly exposed the corruption of the Catholic Church and was well received. The Parish Kirk dates from the 15th century and in the kirkyard a tombstone tells a gruesome story - it is here that the heads of two Covenanters lie buried along with a hand of Hackston of Rathillet who was cruelly executed in Edinburgh in 1680. The Mercat Cross stands near the Town Hall and was brought back from the Hill of Tarvit to mark Queen Victoria's Diamond Jubilee Celebrations.

At Cupar Muir on 13th June, 1559 a volunteer army gathered under the Lords of the Congregation to challenge the Queen Regent's army which was intent on confronting John Knox and the Reformers in St. Andrews. The challenge was effective and a treaty ensured the army withdrew from Fife. A monument on the summit of Hill of Tarvit marks the site of the signing of the treaty.

Left: Mercat Cross in front of the Town Hall, Cupar.

The village of Ceres is attractively grouped around the village green where the oldest Highland Games in Scotland are held every summer. The nearby memorial commemorates the men of Ceres who marched off to Bannockburn to fight against the might of King Edward's army on June 24th, 1314. A 17th century stone bridge crosses the Ceres Burn and it was over this same bridge that Archbishop Sharp passed on his fateful journey to Magus Muir.

The cobbled way over the bridge leads round to the Fife Folk Museum which is located within the 17th century Weigh House and adjoining cottages. Over the doorway a stone carving shows a set of scales with the inscription 'God bless the just.' The museum was opened in 1968 and is run by the Fife Folk Museum Trust. Inside the Museum there is a comprehensive display of crafts, trades, textiles, costumes and implements from the farms and homes in Fife in bygone days.

Beyond the museum is an unusual feature built into a wall. The seated figure resembles a Toby Jug but is actually the Church Provost of 1578 who was the Reverend Thomas Buchanan - the last holder of this post. The Provost was sculpted by John Howie, a local Ceres man.

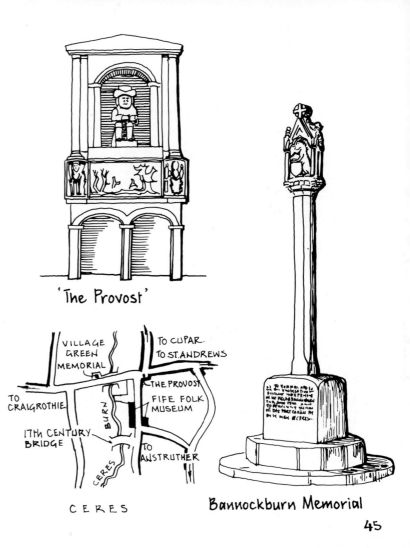

'The Provost'

CERES

Bannockburn Memorial

Scotstarvit Tower

Scotstarvit Tower lies at the top of the Garlie Bank, two miles south of Cupar commanding a view across the Howe of Fife towards the Lomond Hills. It was built for the Inglises of Tarvit in the 1500's and was later bought in 1611 by Sir John Scott of Scotstarvit who added a further storey to the tower. Sir John Scott was acknowledged as one of the great experts of cartography and he published the earliest topographical work on Scotland. With the able assistance of Timothy Pont he surveyed all the counties including the islands of Scotland and had the maps printed in Amsterdam in 1654. Consequently Sir John's accomplishments were widely acknowledged and Scotstarvit Tower became a famous haunt for literary men from all over Europe. One of his most controversial publications was the book — 'The Staggering State of Scots Statesmen' which accused nearly all the Scots statesmen from 1550 - 1650 of gaining public office and wealth by devious means. Not surprisingly the book was not published till long after Scott's death.

Scotstarvit Tower was abandoned in 1696 and was eventually bought by the Wemyss family of Wemysshill House, now known as the Hill of Tarvit Mansion House.

Tarvit Hill Monument

Hill of Tarvit Mansion House

To the east of Scotstarvit Tower is the Hill of Tarvit mansion house. It was built by Sir William Bruce to supercede Scotstarvit Tower and was known as Wemysshall when owned by the Wemyss family. The mansionhouse was practically rebuilt in 1906 by Sir Robert Lorimer for the private collection of paintings, tapestries, porcelains and furniture acquired by Dundee Jute manufacturer Frederick Bower Sharp.

Lorimer was also responsible for the terraced gardens that were designed around the house to enhance the property. Hill of Tarvit mansion house was bequeathed by Frederick Sharp's daughter Elisabeth, to the National Trust for Scotland in 1949. On the summit of Tarvit Hill stands a monument to commemorate the Diamond Jubilee of Queen Victoria in 1897.

47

Coillteach in Gaelic – pronounced culltuch – means a woodland or forest and is normally used in placenames such as Cults. Beyond Pitlessie at Kirkton of Cults is the local Parish Church and manse associated with the famous painter Sir David Wilkie. He was the third son of the Reverend David and Isabella Wilkie and was born in the Cults Manse on 18th November, 1775.

From an early age young David showed a talent for sketching and in 1799 he attended the Edinburgh School of Art. He specialised in capturing the gestures and expressions of people as they enjoyed the attractions of local fairs and markets. In 1804 Wilkie returned to Cults and started on his famous 'Pitlessie Fair' which depicted 140 people. This painting was his stepping stone to fortune, and soon after the Earl of Mansfield commissioned him to paint 'The Village Politicians'. Like many Scots, Wilkie was soon attracted by the bright lights of London and in 1811 he was elected as a member of the Royal Academy.

His fame as a portrait painter brought him high recognition and in 1823 he was appointed as the Kings Limmer (painter) in Scotland; in 1825 he was given the Freedom of the Royal Burgh of Cupar; in 1830 he was appointed Painter in ordinary to King George IV and he was knighted in 1836.

Monument to Sir David Wilkie - Cults Parish Church.

Weathervane near Cults Parish Church.

During a tour of the Far East and the Holy Land he died on board ship on 1st, June, 1841 and was subsequently buried at sea off Cape Trafalgar. Unfortunately the old manse, where Wilkie was born, was destroyed by fire and many of his sketches and paintings were lost. In the Cults Church, however, memorial tablets to both Sir David Wilkie and his parents are mounted on either side of the pulpit. Other notable items in the Church are the old box pews, the Lairds pew, the Lepers' window and the baptisimal font which is a trophy from the Crimea.

Pitlessie, meaning 'garden place' derives from the old Pictish word 'Pit' and the Gaelic 'lios' for garden. This small village, made famous by Wilkie's painting of Pitlessie Fair, still has the old village green and has been a worthy winner of the 'Best Kept Village' Annual Trophy.

Kettle is a Scandinavian forename and settlements such as Kettleshiel in Berwickshire, Kirkettle and Kettleston in the Lothians suggest the presence of Scandinavian settlers. Kingskettle, however, may derive from the Brittonic word 'cuddial' meaning preserve as Kingskettle was located on the edge of the King's hunting preserve of Falkland. Local legend claims that the name comes from 'catel'- a battle - and refers to a great battle between the Scots and Danes before history was recorded.

The Earls of Fife originally owned the lands of Kettle which were later forfeited to the Crown and in a Charter of 1541 the royal prefix of 'Kings' was attached to Kettle. The village of Kingskettle clusters around the Parish Church, which was built in 1832 and replaced an earlier 17th century church. This in turn had replaced an old church dedicated by Bishop de Bernham at Lathrisk in 1243. The nearby village of Kettlebridge began as an early 19th century weavers settlement when the whole parish was involved in the manufacture of shirts and window blinds. The only bridge in the village is at the north end of Mid Street and it is dated 1831. In the days of stagecoach travel 'Kettle' as it is known locally was located on the main route through Fife between the ferry ports of Pettycur and Newport-on-Tay.

Kettle Parish Church

49

Ladybank

In the early days Ladybank was surrounded by extensive marshlands and was aptly known as Ladybog by the monks of Lindores Abbey. During the 13th century the monks were granted permission by a local laird - Roger de Quince 'to take two hundred loads of heather and peat from these marshlands. The village prospered as a small weaving settlement in the early 19th century and its importance increased with the building of the railway line through Fife. Ladybank as it now became known was a main railway junction on the Edinburgh to Perth and Dundee lines and by 1878 the village had been made a burgh. On the sporting front the Ladybank Golf Club was founded in 1879 and is used as a qualifying course when the Open is played at St. Andrews. In 1921 the Howe of Fife Rugby Football Club was formed at Ladybank and in 1946 the 'Howe' amalgamated with Cupar RFC.

Main Street, Dunshalt

The small village of Dunshalt lies on the road between Auchtermuchty and Falkland. The meaning of Dunshalt is unknown. Perhaps it was known as the Danes Hold or Halt because it was here that the Danes had chosen to camp after fleeing from their defeat on Falkland Moor. Or maybe Dunshalt derives From the Gaelic 'dun' meaning fort and 'sealg' meaning hunt and pronounced 'shalg' giving 'hunting fort.' Given the vicinity of Falkland Palace and the abundance of hunting that went on for deer and boar in the Howe of Fife there are convincing reasons for believing this interpretation.

51

Falkland, situated in the shadow of the East Lomond Hill, was the favourite residence of the Stewart monarchy and was consequently made a Royal Burgh by James II in 1458. Originally, Macduff the Thane of Fife had built a castle at Falkland which was acquired by the Stewarts in the 14th century. From then on it became a Palace - a place for entertainment and recreation, for the Royal Family and its entourage, as they indulged in hunting boar and deer; went hawking with the use of trained falcons and took part in the more peaceful pursuit of Royal Tennis at the specially made enclosed court in the Palace grounds.

More sinister events haunted the Palace, however, and in 1402 the Palace was the scene of the cruel starvation and murder of the Duke of Rothsay, (the heir to the throne) by the Duke of Albany. In 1542 James V died here and on being told that the Queen had given birth at Linlithgow Palace to a daughter, Mary, Queen of Scots he prophesied just before his death - 'It cam wi' a lass, it will gang wi' a lass.' He was refering to the fact that Marjorie Bruce, the daughter of Robert the Bruce, married Walter Stewart in 1315 thus bringing the House of Stewart into the Royal Family. James V prophecy, however did not come true until the death of Queen Anne in 1714.

The Gatehouse, Falkland Palace.

FALKLAND

$\mathbb{F}$alkland naturally thrived with the Royal presence but after the Union of the Crowns in 1603 Royal visits decreased and the Palace fell into decay in the early 1700's. The arrival of a major benefactor, Onesiphorus Tyndall-Bruce in the early 1800's resulted in great improvements including the building of the House of Falkland, the Bruce Fountain and the rebuilding of the Parish Church. Tyndall-Bruce's wife had inherited the Falkland Estate from her uncle and in 1887 the estate passed to John Crichton-Stuart, the Third Marquess of Bute. In his position as Hereditary Keeper of the Palace he organised a thorough restoration of the Palace buildings. Today the Palace is still owned by the reigning monarch with the National Trust for Scotland acting as Deputy Keeper since 1952.

Falkland Palace

53

Horsemarket, Falkland

Over the centuries the spinning and weaving of local flax created a thriving cottage industry but by the end of the 18th century the power loom had virtually replaced the handweavers. Other industries involving the manufacture of linen cloth and linoleum replaced the weaving industry but had petered out by the 1970's.

Today Falkland relies heavily on the Palace which is a major tourist attraction and the town caters admirably for this new industry with craft shops and tea rooms. The older area of Falkland has been recognised as being of great historical and architectural interest and has consequently been designated a Conservation area to ensure the character of the town is retained.

A walk around Falkland will reveal many interesting buildings and streets. Horsemarket would cater for the horse trading which would take place on a weekly basis and at the annual fairs as stipulated in the charters. The house at the corner of Back Wynd and Horsemarket has an excellent example of a forestair. This is a traditional method of gaining access to the First Floor and is one of the few surviving examples still to be seen in the area.

In Brunton Street there is a coat of arms of the Simson Family over a window to Brunton House. They were the hereditary falconers to the Crown. Running down to the High Street is the cobbled Rottenrow, a reminder of the street surfaces of yesteryear before the invention of tar macadam. At the foot of Rottenrow stands another two storey house with a fore stair and it is a peculiar example of conservation as it is now used as an Electricity Sub-Station. Further along the High Street is Cameron House, the birthplace of Covenanter Richard Cameron who was killed at the Battle of Aird Moss in 1680.

In the Square is the Bruce Fountain and nearby a cobbled cross in the road marks the site of the Mercat Cross. The Parish Church, built in 1850, faces into the Square with the Town Hall and the Burgh crest standing opposite. The National Trust for Scotland bought the Town Hall in 1986 and also restored the three houses alongside the Palace. Marriage lintels with the initials of the couple and the date of marriage may be seen over the doorways. Opposite are two 17th century houses – Moncrieff House with its thatched roof and the Hunting Lodge Hotel with its decorated panels. Finally the impressive Gatehouse to the Palace, which was built in 1541, dominates the street scene and it is well worth visiting the Palace to see the Royal Chapel, the Royal Tennis Court and Palace Gardens.

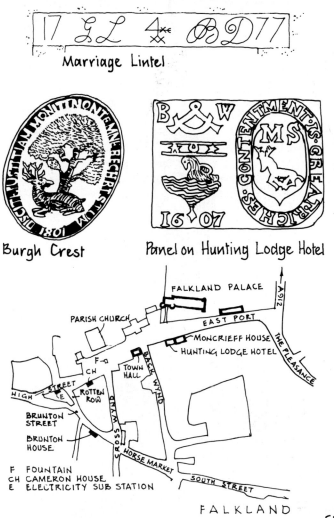

Marriage Lintel

Burgh Crest

Panel on Hunting Lodge Hotel

F FOUNTAIN
CH CAMERON HOUSE
E ELECTRICITY SUB STATION

FALKLAND

55

Strathmiglo is a 16th century Burgh of Barony with two distinct districts of Kirklands and Templelands which acknowledged the division of lands in the 15th century between the Church and Knights Templars. James V granted the lands of Cairnie, (Wester Strathmiglo) to Sir William Scott of Balwearie. In order that Sir William could entertain the King, who was often in residence at Falkland Palace he built a castle at Cairnie. The Castle was hastily built and accordingly was nicknamed Cairnie Flappit. By 1734 the Castle lay in ruins but the stones were put to good use in the building of the Town Hall Steeple in the High Street. The Steeple originally had a prison at ground floor level and the outside stair led to the mid 19th century Town Hall on the first floor.

Close by are the headquarters of the famous firm - Hoggs, Fife Footwear Co. established by A.T. Hogg in 1888. Hoggs are known worldwide for their boots and brogues and it was A.T. Hogg who originally had the idea of selling boots through the post. Further along the High Street is a most unusual right of way which leads through a passage in the Strathmiglo Inn to the Back Dykes. In the heyday of the weaving industry there were two factories in Strathmiglo but by the early 1960's the sole surviving factory in Skene Street had closed down. The factory was then used by the Irvine Thread Company until its closure in 1996.

Town Hall Steeple, Strathmiglo.

Auchtermuchty became a Royal Burgh in 1517 and derives its name from a Pictish settlement - uachdarmuc - meaning "high ground of the wild boar." Chaos reigned in the town in 1818 when the burgh was declared bankrupt. Consequently the magistrates were thrown in jail while the assets of the Burgh were sold to pay the creditors. Until the 19th century Auchtermuchty was renowned for its weaving industry and more recently for light engineering and the first commercial red deer farm in the UK. which is situated at nearby Reedie Hill. The Town House forms a prominent landmark in the market place, which is known as the Cross, although today it is the War Memorial that stands in the place of the old Mercat Cross. Further along the High Street is Macduff House which was built in the 1590's and is the oldest house in the town. Finally, Auchtermuchty is the home of that great accordian player, Jimmy Shand.

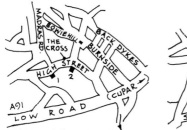

1. MACDUFF HOUSE.   FALKLAND
2. TOWN HALL
AUCHTERMUCHTY

STRATHMIGLO

Town Hall

High Street, Freuchie

58

The Gaelic word for heather is fraoch - roughly pronounced as 'freeugh' and in its anglicised spelling is rendered as Freuchie. Local legend maintains that members of the Royal Court at Falkland who were out of favour were told to go "Awa tae Freuchie" to cool their heels. This may well have been the case as the village of Freuchie lies a few miles east of Falkland. Between these two villages lies Newton of Falkland — famous for its brewing and malting in days gone by. Today the old brewery buildings have been converted into flats.

In 1985 Freuchie gained National fame when the Freuchie Cricket Club won the National Village Championships at Lords. The village has also deservedly won the best kept village 'small town section' annual trophy several times.

Freuchie - with East Lomond hill in the background.

59

West Lomond Hill

Gateside was formerly known as Edenshead due to its location near the source of the River Eden that runs through the flat fertile valley known as the Howe of Fife. The Ochil Hills lie to the north west but it is the nearby Lomond Hills that hold an elusive secret. Local folklore insists that the West Lomond was the scene of an ancient battle between the invading Romans and 30,000 Britons under Calgacus. Since then human remains and burnt bones have been unearthed by the banks of the River Eden to substantiate this claim. This is hotly disputed, however, by historians who maintain that Tacitus recorded a battle in 85 AD which was fought on a hill called Mons Grapius, north of the River Tay - not near the Lomond Hills. The East Lomond (448m) shows traces of an ancient Pictish fort dating back at least 1500 years and on the north slopes of the West Lomond (552m) stands the Bannet Stane - an odd shaped stone balanced on an outcrop of rocks. Its significance is unknown but it may well be an ancient altar for sunworshippers or a Pictish King's tombstone. The Maiden's Bower is a cave in these same rocks where a young girl lived the life of a hermit after her lover was killed by her father's servants. In the 18th century lead and silver were mined on the East Lomond and in 1852 a gold rush on the West Lomond quickly petered out. Finally, the Gateside Mills are renowned for the manufacture of wooden bases for figurines and also textile bobbins which are exported worldwide.

The houses and cottages of Collessie are scattered around the 19th century Parish Church which sits high above the Howe of Fife. Until the 1750's Rossie Loch would have flooded the Howe and in earlier days the monks of nearby Lindores Abbey used to cut peat turfs from the marshes. Legend maintains that James V, disguised as the 'Gudeman of Ballangeich' would often wander in the Collessie area while staying at Falkland Palace. This allowed him to make intimate acquaintance with his subjects who were often unaware of the true identity of the stranger in their midst. Like many Fife villages Collessie has several 18th and 19th century weavers cottages and one cottage still has a thatched roof with a sundial carved into the skewputt. Today Collessie is a Conservation area and several houses and cottages have been restored including one which houses a Pictish collection.

In this area of the Howe of Fife some ancient mounds indicate the site of old forts. In 1876 a burial cairn dating back to the Bronze Age was excavated at Gask Hill. The cairn occupied an area of about forty metres in diameter and contained many decorated urns and old bones. To the south of Collessie is Birnie Loch nature reserve created from the restored workings of Kinloch Quarry and donated to the people of Fife by J.S. Baird & Sons and Pioneer Aggregates UK Ltd in 1991. Near the loch is the Ostrich Kingdom with its ostrich farm and unusual animal collection.

Collessie

61

Town House, Newburgh.

Newburgh lies to the north of Fife overlooking the River Tay. It was made a burgh of barony in 1266 and confirmed as a Royal Burgh in 1631. In the early 19th century Newburgh was a key base for the summer salmon fishing and along with the weaving industry provided gainful employment. In 1891 a linoleum factory was built but recently closed in 1978. The history of the area is on display at the Laing Museum which opened in 1896 and was named after Dr. Alexander Laing. Of particular interest are Laings antique collection, a display of Australasian artifacts and information gleaned on the ancient Pictish hillfort at Clachard.

The nearby Lindores Abbey was founded in 1178 for the Benedictine Order by David, Earl of Huntingdon and it is now a fragmented ruin. In 1300 Sir William Wallace celebrated victory here after defeating the English on the nearby field of Black Earnside. Later in 1402, the young Duke of Rothsay was buried in the Abbey after his cruel death at Falkland. The ultimate fate of the Abbey was sealed when it came under attack from the zealous reformers in 1543 and 1559 and thereafter gradually fell into ruin as the stone was used in local buildings.

Two ancient crosses stand near Newburgh. There is the four metre high Celtic Cross of Mugdrum which has stood for over 1300 years. The story of the Cross is lost in the past and the only surviving carvings of constant erosion show hunters on horseback chasing wild boar. The other cross is associated with Macduff but only the base now remains. The legend claims that the Macduff Clan could seek sanctuary at the Cross if they were guilty of murder but historians strongly dispute this.

The Author

John MacMillan Pearson was born at St. Andrews in 1952. He is an architect by profession having graduated with a Bachelor of Architecture degree at Heriot-Watt University, Edinburgh in 1976. Travelled overseas between 1977-1983 to Canada, Mexico and the Far East and worked in New Zealand and Australia before returning to Scotland. Developed a keen interest in sketching and calligraphy through meeting the Canadian artist Barbara Elizabeth Mercer. From 1983-1987 he worked for the Edinburgh architects' firm Dick Peddie & McKay at their branch office in Invergordon. Following a six year spell in London area, while working on an office development for Grosvenor Developments at Harrow, he returned to Scotland in 1993 and is now based at Perth working on a self employed basis.

"Old Pudding Bag Cottage"
John M. Pearson

For a black and white pen and ink sketch of your house or a pen and ink sketch tinted with watercolour - contact: John Pearson
Lingmoor, Carberry Park, Leven, Fife.
tel. 01333 426248 / 01738 635118

List of publications by John M. Pearson

A Guided Walk round Inverness
A Guided Walk round Edinburgh
Edinburgh Old Town Pilgrims' Way (text: D. Smith)
Series on Kingdom of Fife :—
'Around North East Fife'
Around Kirkcaldy
Around Dunfermline'
A Guided Walk round St. Andrews
Burntisland
Around Stirling
Around Perthshire
Maps : St Andrews Street map
       Edinburgh Royal Mile Guide
       Old Town Pilgrims' Way
       Alexander Selkirk - (the real Robinson Crusoe)

BIBLIOGRAPHY

About St. Andrews and About by James K. Robertson
Discovering Fife by Raymond Lamont-Brown
A Falkland Guide by the Falkland Society
Falkland Points of View by the Falkland Society
Hill of Tarvit - National Trust for Scotland
Kellie Castle - National Trust for Scotland
Seatoun of Largo by Ivy Jardine.
The Buildings of Scotland - Fife by John Gifford
The Kingdom of Fife by Theo Lang
The Kingdom of Fife by Glen L. Pride
The Lion in the North by John Prebble
The Story of Upper Largo Kirk by Rev. D. Lister & J. Gillies